THE GUITAR COLLECTION

MOVIE SONGS

64 Popular Songs from Memorable Films

Produced by
Alfred Music
P.O. Box 10003
Van Nuys, CA 91410-0003
alfred.com

Printed in USA.

ISBN-10: 1-4706-3244-6
ISBN-13: 978-1-4706-3244-1

 Alfred Cares. Contents printed on environmentally responsible paper.

CONTENTS

MOVIE INDEX

AGAINST ALL ODDS
(Take a Look at Me Now)

*To match recording, Capo 1

Words and Music by
PHIL COLLINS

*Recording sounds a half step higher than written.

Verse:

1. How can I just let___ you walk a-way, just let you leave with-out___ a trace? When I
2.3. *See additional lyrics*

stand here tak - ing ev - 'ry breath___ with you;___ ooh.___ You're the

on - ly one who real - ly knew me___ at all.___

Chorus 1 & 2:

So take a look at me now,___ well, there's just an

Take a look at me now.

Verse 2:
How can you just walk away from me,
When all I can do is watch you leave?
'Cause you shared the laughter and the pain,
And even shared the tears.
You're the only one who really knew me at all.
(To Chorus 1:)

Verse 3:
I wish I could just make you turn around,
Turn around and see me cry.
There's so much I need to say to you,
So many reasons why.
You're the only one who really knew me at all.
(To Chorus 2:)

ARTHUR'S THEME
(BEST THAT YOU CAN DO)

(from *Arthur*)

Words and Music by
BURT BACHARACH, CAROLE BAYER SAGER,
CHRISTOPHER CROSS and PETER ALLEN

Moderately slow, with half-time feel (♩ = 68) (♩ = 136)

1. Once in your life___ you'll find___ her, some-one who turns___ your heart a-round and
2. Ar-thur he does___ as he pleas-es. All of his life,___ he's mas-ter's toys, and

next thing you know,___ you're clos-in' down the town.___
deep in his heart___ he's just, he's just a boy.___

Arthur's Theme (Best That You Can Do) - 2 - 1

BATMAN THEME

Moderately fast ♩ = 158

Words and Music by
NEAL HEFTI

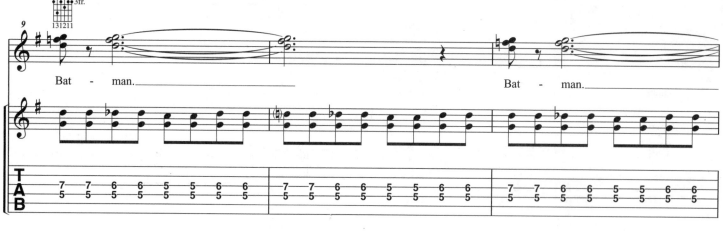

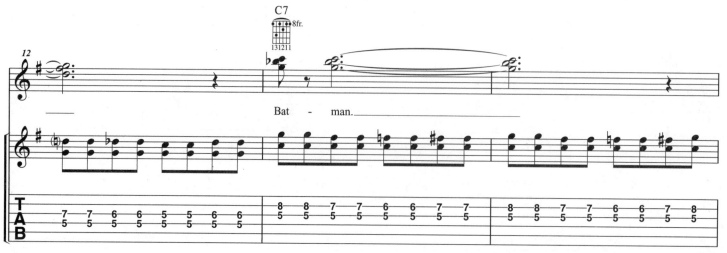

Batman Theme - 2 - 1

BECAUSE YOU LOVED ME

(Theme from *Up Close and Personal*)

*To match recording, Capo I

Words and Music by
DIANE WARREN

*Recording sounds a half step higher than written.

Because You Loved Me - 4 - 1

BELIEVE

(from *The Polar Express*)

Words and Music by
ALAN SILVESTRI and GLEN BALLARD

Moderately slow ♩ = 80

1. Chil - dren sleep - ing, snow is soft - ly fall - ing.
2. Trains move quick - ly to their jour - ney's end.

Dreams are call - ing like bells in the dis - tance.
Des - ti - na - tions are where we be - gin a - gain.

We were dream - ers, not so long a - go,
Ships go sail - ing far a - cross the sea,

but one by one, we all had to grow up.
trust - ing star - light to get where they need to be.

When it seems the mag - ic slipped a - way, we find it all a - gain on Christ - mas
When it seems that we have lost our way, we find our - selves a - gain on Christ - mas

Day. Be - Day. Be -

Believe - 2 - 1

BLUE VELVET

Moderately slow ♩ = 82

Words and Music by
LEE MORRIS and BERNIE WAYNE

Blue Velvet - 2 - 1

Verse 3:
But when she left, gone was the glow of blue velvet.
But in my heart there'll always be precious and warm memories through the years.
And I still can see blue velvet through my tears.
(To Verse 4:)

Blue Velvet - 2 - 2

CONCERNING HOBBITS

(from The Lord of the Rings: The Fellowship of the Ring)

By HOWARD SHORE

Concerning Hobbits - 6 - 1

Concerning Hobbits - 6 - 6

EVERGREEN

(Love Theme from *A Star Is Born*)

Words by PAUL WILLIAMS
Music by BARBRA STREISAND

Moderately ♩ = 115
Intro:

*Sung on repeat only.

Evergreen - 5 - 1

EVERYTHING IS AWESOME
(Awesome Remixxx!!!)
(from The Lego Movie)

Lyrics by
SHAWN PATTERSON, ANDY SAMBERG,
AKIVA SCHAFFER, JORMA TACCONE,
JOSHUA BARTHOLOMEW and LISA HARRITON

Music by
SHAWN PATTERSON

Everything Is Awesome (Awesome Remixxx!!!) - 3 - 1

Rap section 1:
Have you heard the news, everyone's talking
Life is good 'cause everything's awesome
Lost my job, it's a new opportunity
More free time for my awesome community.

I feel more awesome than an awesome possum
Dip my body in chocolate frostin'
Three years later, wash off the frostin'
Smellin' like a blossom, everything is awesome
Stepped in mud, got new brown shoes
It's awesome to win, and it's awesome to lose (it's awesome to lose).

Rap section 2:
Blue skies, bouncy springs
We just named two awesome things
A Nobel prize, a piece of string
You know what's awesome? EVERYTHING!

Dogs with fleas, allergies,
A book of Greek antiquities
Brand new pants, a very old vest
Awesome items are the best.

Trees, frogs, clogs
They're awesome
Rocks, clocks, and socks
They're awesome
Figs, and jigs, and twigs
That's awesome
Everything you see, or think, or say
Is awesome.

EVERYTHING I DO (I DO IT FOR YOU)

*To match record key, Capo I

Words and Music by
BRYAN ADAMS,
ROBERT JOHN "MUTT" LANGE
and MICHAEL KAMEN

Slowly ♩ = 66

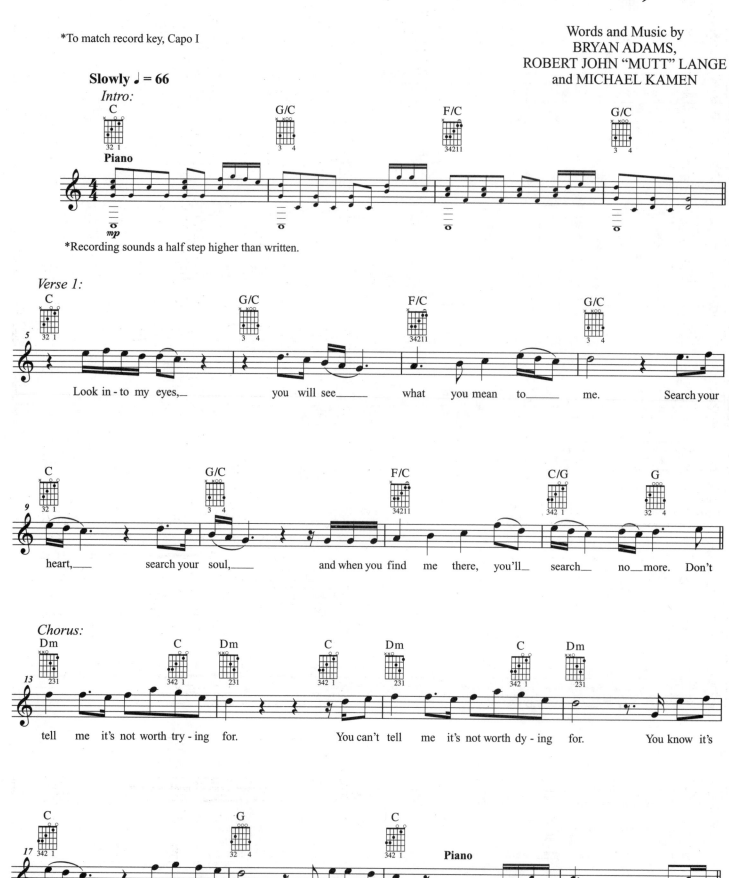

Everything I Do (I Do It for You) - 4 - 1

Everything I Do (I Do It for You) - 4 - 4

FALLING SLOWLY

(from *Once*)

Words and Music by
GLEN HANSARD and MARKETA IRGLOVA

Falling Slowly - 3 - 1

FOOTLOOSE

Words by
DEAN PITCHFORD

Music by
KENNY LOGGINS

*All gtrs. Capo I or tuned up 1/2 step:

⑥ = F   ③ = A♭
⑤ = B♭   ② = C
④ = E♭   ① = F

Moderately fast ♩ = 174
Intro:

A

Elec. Gtr. 1 *(clean-tone)*
Riff A

end Riff A

*Recording sounds a half step higher than written.

A7

Elec. Gtr. 2 *(w/partial dist.)*

trem. bar

Elec. Gtr. 1

Footloose - 8 - 1

Verse:

Elec.
Gtrs.
1 & 2

A5

Elec.
Gtr. 2
dbld. by
Keybd.

D   A

1. Been work - ing___ so hard,___ I'm punch - ing___
2. You're play - ing___ so cool,___ o - bey - ing___

*Composite arrangement.

Chorus:

loose,___ foot - loose. Kick off my Sun - day shoes.
loose,___ foot - loose. Kick off my Sun - day shoes. Oo,

Elec. Gtr. 3 *(clean-tone) dbld. by Bass Gtr.*

mf

Please, Lou - ise, pull me off of my knees.
wee, Ma - rie, shake it, shake it for me.

Jack, get back, come___ on be - fore we crack.
Oh, Mi - lo, come___ on, come on, let's go.

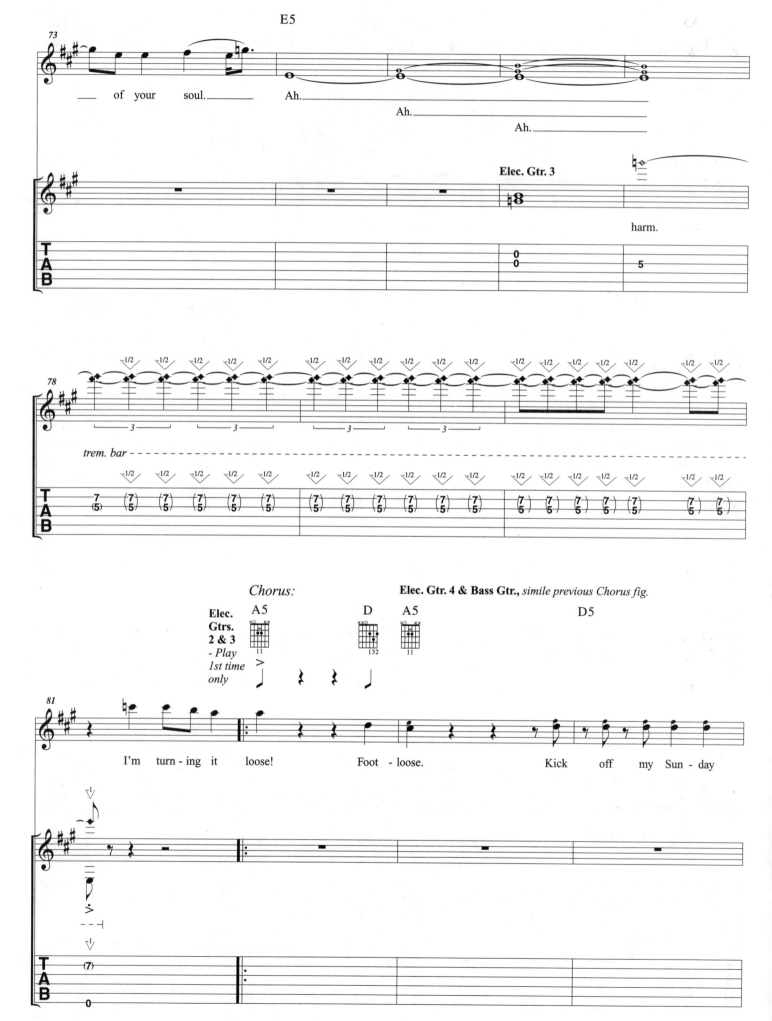

shoes. Please, Lou - ise, pull me off of my knees.

Jack, get back, come__ on be - fore we crack.

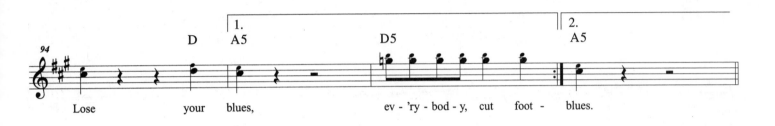

Lose your blues, ev - 'ry - bod - y, cut foot - blues.

Outro:

Ev - 'ry - bod - y, cut, ev - 'ry - bod - y cut.__ Ev - 'ry - bod - y, cut, ev - 'ry -

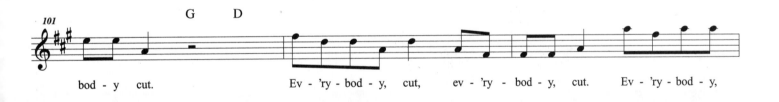

bod - y cut. Ev - 'ry - bod - y, cut, ev - 'ry - bod - y, cut. Ev - 'ry - bod - y,

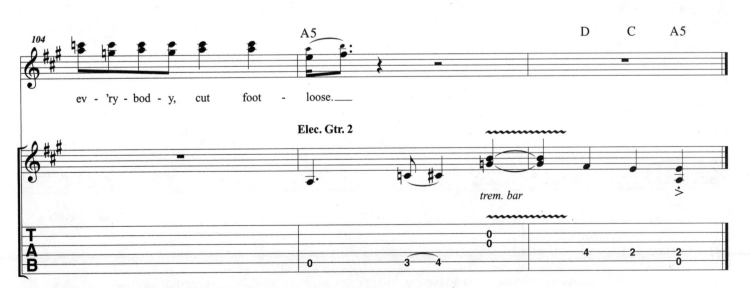

ev - 'ry - bod - y, cut foot - loose.__

Elec. Gtr. 2

trem. bar

Footloose - 8 - 8

FOR YOUR EYES ONLY

(from *For Your Eyes Only*)

Lyrics by
MICHAEL LEESON

Music by
BILL CONTI

Moderately slow ♩ = 82

Intro:

§ Verse:

your eyes on - ly can see me through the night. For
your eyes on - ly, the nights are nev - er cold. You

your eyes on - ly I nev - er need to hide. I
real - ly know me, that's all I need to know. But

You can see so much in me, so much in me that's new.
May - be I'm an o - pen book, be - cause I know you're mine.

nev - er felt un - til I looked at you. For your eyes
you won't need to read be - tween the lines.

For Your Eyes Only - 2 - 1

GHOSTBUSTERS

Moderately ♩ = 116

Words and Music by
RAY PARKER, JR.

Ghost - bust - ers!

1. If there's

Ghostbusters - 6 - 1

56

58

Ghostbusters - 6 - 5

GONNA FLY NOW
(Theme from *Rocky*)

Words and Music by
BILL CONTI, AYN ROBBINS
and CAROL CONNORS

Try-in' hard now._____

Gonna Fly Now - 3 - 1

It's so hard now._____ Try-in' hard now._____

Guitar Solo:

8va throughout
Elec. Gtr. *(w/dist.)*

Elec. Gtr. resume rhy. simile

dist. off

GLORY OF LOVE
(Theme from *The Karate Kid, Part II*)

Words and Music by
DAVID FOSTER, PETER CETERA
and DIANE NINI

Glory of Love - 6 - 1

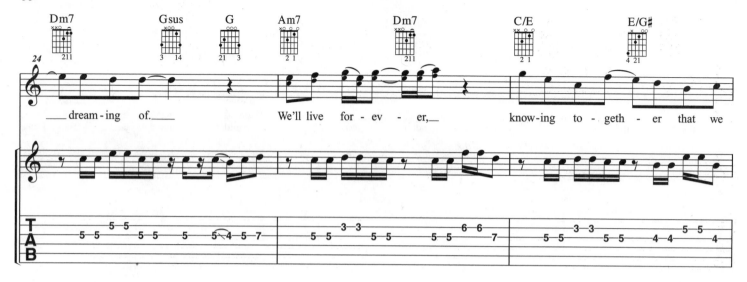

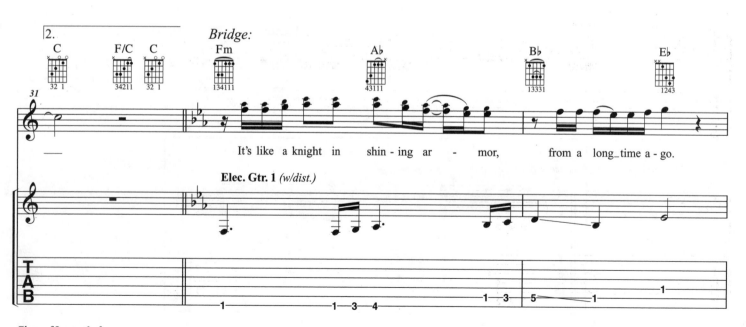

Glory of Love - 6 - 6

GOLDFINGER

(from *Goldfinger*)

Lyrics by
**LESLIE BRICUSSE and
ANTHONY NEWLEY**

Music by
JOHN BARRY

THE GOOD, THE BAD AND THE UGLY
(Main Title)

By
ENNIO MORRICONE

The Good, the Bad and the Ugly - 2 - 1

The Good, the Bad and the Ugly - 2 - 2

THE GREATEST LOVE OF ALL

*To match recording, Capo I

Words by LINDA CREED
Music by MICHAEL MASSER

*Recording sounds a half step higher than written.
**Intro chords implied by piano.

Verses 1–3:

1.3. I be-lieve the chil-dren are our fu - ture.   Teach them well__ and let__ them lead__ the way.
2. *See additional lyrics*

Show them all the beau - ty they pos-sess in - side.__   Give them a

sense__ of pride__ to make it eas - i - er.__   Let the chil-drens' laugh ter re-

The Greatest Love of All - 4 - 1

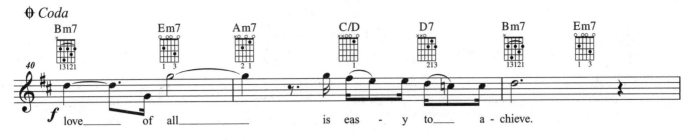

love____ of all_____ is eas - y to____ a - chieve.

Learn - ing to love your - self____ is the great - est love of____ all. And if by____ chance, that

Verse 4:

spe - cial place that you've____ been dream-ing of leads you to a

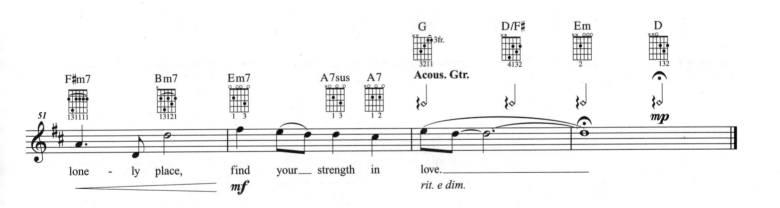

lone - ly place, find your____ strength in love.____

Verse 2:
Everybody's searching for a hero.
People need someone to look up to.
I never found anyone who fulfilled my needs.
A lonely place to be, so I learned to depend on me.
(To Pre-chorus:)

HAIR
(from *Hair*)

Words by
JAMES RADO and GEROME RAGNI

Music by
GALT MacDERMOT

Hair - 4 - 1

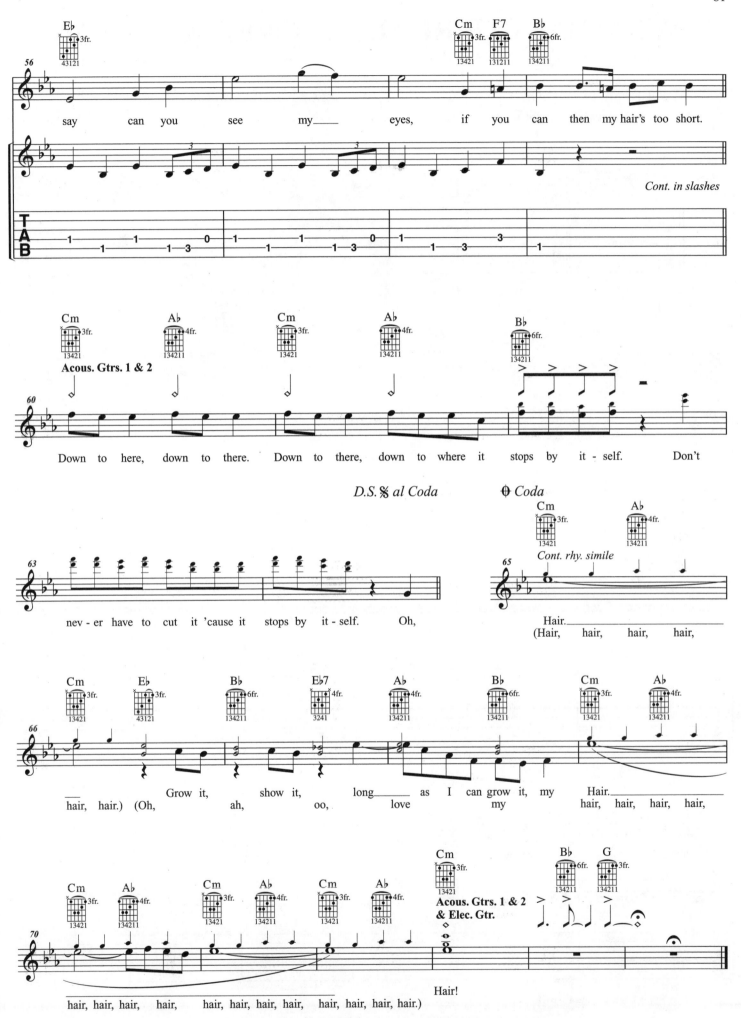

Hair - 4 - 4

HAVE YOU EVER REALLY LOVED A WOMAN?

Lyrics by
**BRYAN ADAMS and
ROBERT JOHN "MUTT" LANGE**

Music by
MICHAEL KAMEN

Moderately bright waltz ♩ = 146

Intro:

Have You Ever Really Loved a Woman? - 6 - 1

HAVE YOURSELF A MERRY LITTLE CHRISTMAS

Words and Music by
HUGH MARTIN and RALPH BLANE

HOW DO I LIVE

Words and Music by
DIANE WARREN

Moderately slow ♩ = 72

Verse:

get through one night with-out___ you?___ If I had to

live with-out___ you,___ what kind of life would that be?___ Oh,___ I,___ I need you in my

arms, need you__ to hold.___ You're my world, my heart,__ my soul.___ If you ev - er leave,___

ba - by, you would take a - way___ ev - 'ry-thing__ good in my life.___ And tell me

Chorus:

now, how do I live with - out___ you? I want to know.___ How do I breathe with - out___

How Do I Live - 3 - 1

To Coda ⊕

Verse 2:
Without you, there'd be no sun in my sky,
There would be no love in my life,
There'd be no world left for me.
And I, baby, I don't know what I would do,
I'd be lost if I lost you.
If you ever leave,
Baby, you would take away everything real in my life.

And tell me now,
(To Chorus:)

HIGH NOON
(Do Not Forsake Me, Oh My Darlin')
Main Title

Words by
NED WASHINGTON

Music by
DIMITRI TIOMKIN

High Noon (Do Not Forsake Me, Oh My Darlin') - 2 - 1

HIgh Noon (Do Not Forsake Me, Oh My Darlin') - 2 - 2

I DON'T WANT TO MISS A THING

(from *Armageddon*)

Words and Music by
DIANE WARREN

*Chord frames are suggested.

I Don't Want to Miss a Thing - 5 - 1

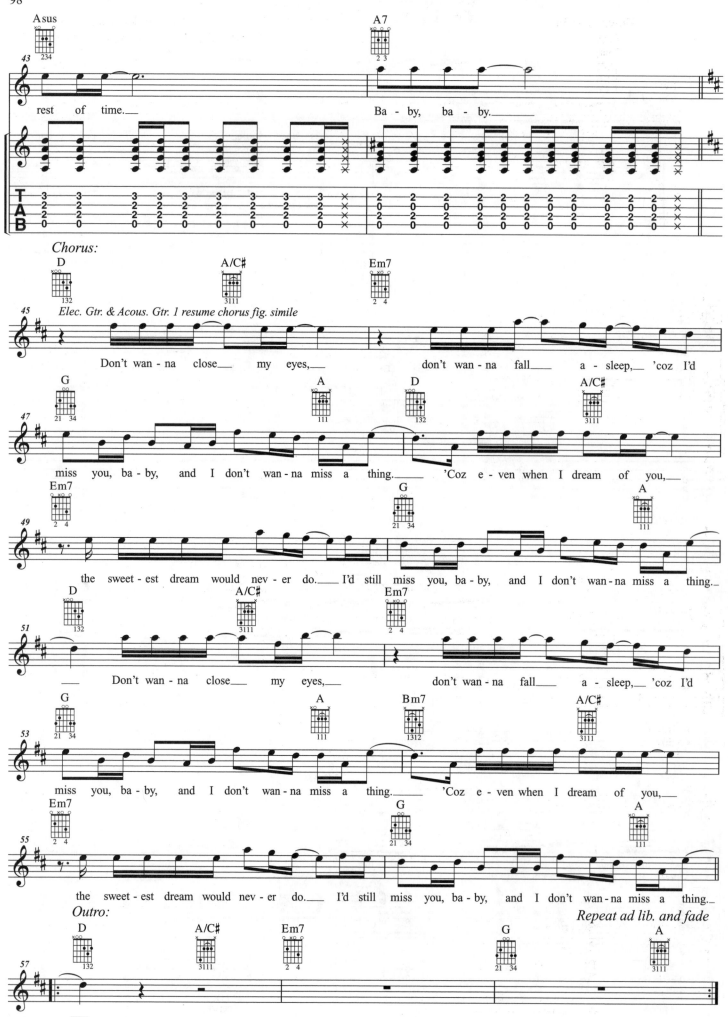

I HAVE NOTHING

Words and Music by
LINDA THOMPSON and DAVID FOSTER

I LOVE TO SEE YOU SMILE

Words and Music by
RANDY NEWMAN

I Love to See You Smile - 2 - 1

Verse 2:
Don't want to take a trip to China.
Don't want to sail up the Nile.
Wouldn't want to get too far from where you are
'Cause I love to see you smile.

Verse 3:
(Instrumental)

Verse 4:
Like a sink without a faucet,
Like a watch without a dial,
What would I do if I didn't have you?
I love to see you smile.
(To Bridge:)

I SEE FIRE

*To match recording, Capo VI

Words and Music by
ED SHEERAN

*Recording sounds three whole steps higher than written.

I See Fire - 6 - 1

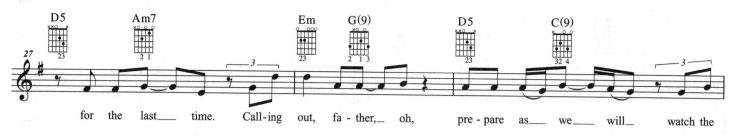

for the last___ time. Call-ing out, fa - ther,___ oh, pre - pare as___ we___ will___ watch the

flames burn au - burn on_____ the moun - tain side.___ Des - o - la - tion comes___ up - on the sky.___

Chorus:

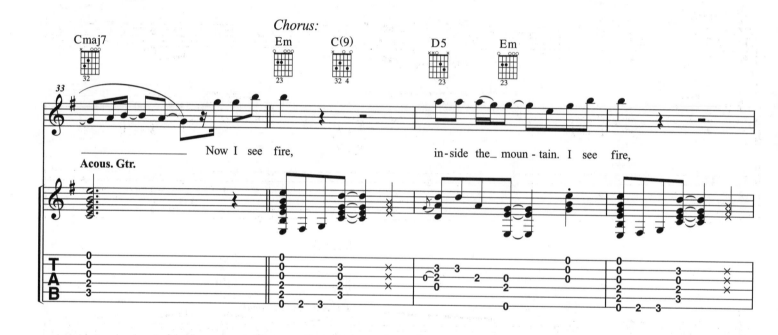

Now I see fire, in-side the___ moun - tain. I see fire,

Acous. Gtr.

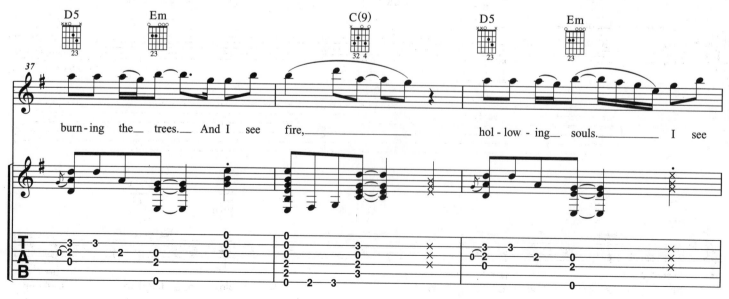

burn-ing the___ trees. And I see fire,_____ hol - low - ing___ souls._____ I see

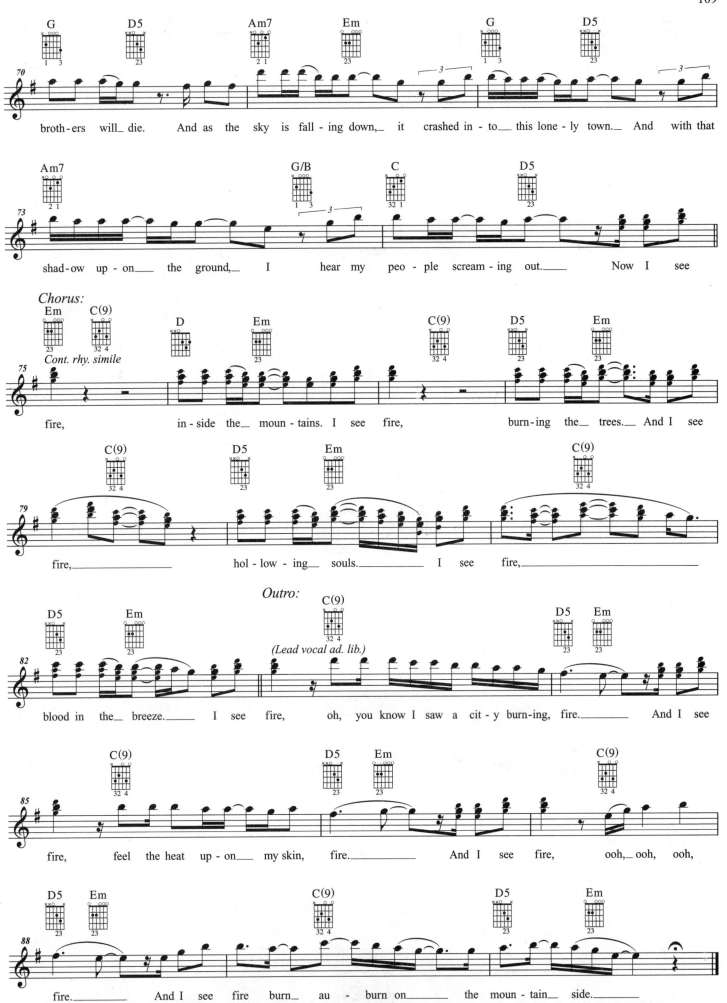

I'M ALRIGHT

(from *Caddyshack*)

Words and Music by
KENNY LOGGINS

*Elec. Gtr. 1 in Drop D tuning:
⑥ = D   ③ = G
⑤ = A   ② = B
④ = D   ① = E

Moderately in 2 ♩ = 82
Chorus:

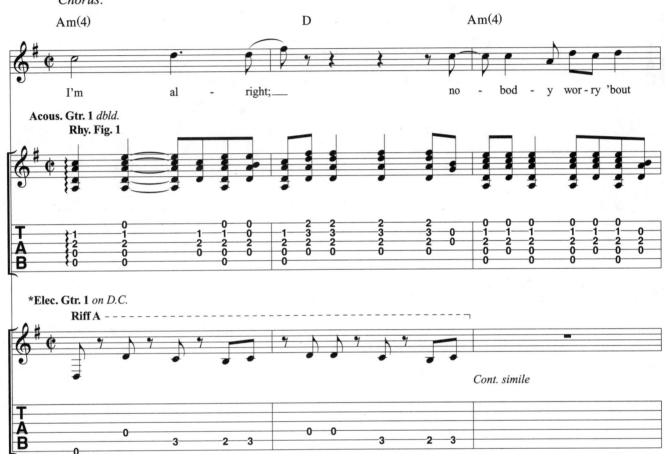

I'm al - right;___ no - bod - y wor-ry 'bout

Acous. Gtr. 1 *dbld.*
Rhy. Fig. 1

*Elec. Gtr. 1 on D.C.
Riff A
Cont. simile

w/Rhy. Fig. 1 *(Acous. Gtr. 1) 2 3/4 times, simile*

me.   Why___ you got to gim - me a fight?___   Can't___ you just let it be?___

end Rhy. Fig. 1

I'm Alright - 5 - 1

Verse:

- in', _____ own _____ heart _____ beat - in', _____ own _____ heart _____ beat -

Pre-chorus:

Elec.
Gtr. 3
*(w/dist.
& flanger
effect)*

A5

- in'. _____ Own _____ heart. _____ Yeah. _____

"Got - ta
Don't it

catch you lat - er." _____ "No, _____ no, can - non - ball it right a - way." _____
get you mov - in'? M - m - m - m - man, it makes me feel good. _____

G5

Get it up and get you a job. _____

Some _____ Cin - der - el - la kid. _____

1.   *D.C. al Coda*   2.

Duh, duh, duh, duh, duh, duh, duh, duh.   Duh, duh, duh, duh, duh, duh, duh, duh.

I'm.

Boom, boom, boom.

Outro Chorus:
w/Rhy. Fig. 1 *(Acous. Gtr. 1) 4 times, simile*
w/Riff A *(Elec. Gtr. 1) 8 times, simile*

I'm al - right;___ No - bod - y wor - ry 'bout me. Why___

2nd Vocal: I'm al - right._____

___ you got to gim - me a fight?___ Can't___ you just let it be?___

I'm al - right;___ don't___

I'm al - right;___

no - bod - y wor - ry 'bout me. You___ got to gim - me a

don't no - bod - y wor - ry 'bout.

Repeat ad lib. to fade

fight?___ Why don't___ you just let me be?

Why you wan - na fight? Don't you let___ me.___

I'm Alright - 5 - 5

INTO THE WEST

(from *The Lord of the Rings: The Return of the King*)

*To match record key, Capo III:

Moderately ♩ = 92

Words and Music by
HOWARD SHORE, FRAN WALSH
and ANNIE LENNOX

*Recording sounds a minor 3rd higher than written.

Into the West - 4 - 1

IT MIGHT BE YOU
(Theme from *Tootsie*)

Words by
ALAN and MARILYN BERGMAN

Music by
DAVE GRUSIN

Moderately ♩ = 90

It Might Be You - 2 - 1

It Might Be You - 2 - 2

JAMES BOND THEME

By MONTY NORMAN

James Bond Theme - 3 - 1

124

James Bond Theme - 3 - 3

LET IT GO

(from Walt Disney's *Frozen*)

Music and Lyrics by
KRISTEN ANDERSON-LOPEZ
and ROBERT LOPEZ

*To match record key, Capo I

Moderately, with a half-time feel ♩ = 137

Intro:

*Recording sounds a half step higher than written.

The

Verse 1:

snow glows white on the moun-tain to-night,__ not a foot-print__ to be seen.__ A

Cont. rhy. simile

king-dom of i-so-la-tion, and it looks like I'm the queen.__

The wind__ is howl-ing like__ this swirl-ing storm in-side.

Let It Go - 5 - 1

Let It Go - 5 - 3

LIVE AND LET DIE

Words and Music by
PAUL McCARTNEY and
LINDA McCARTNEY

Slowly ♩ = 60
Verse:

1. When you were young and your heart was an o-pen book.
2. *Instrumental*

You used to say live and let live. (You know you did, you know you did, you know you did.____) But if this ev-er chang-ing world in which we live in makes you give it a cry,____ say live and let die!____ Live and let die,____ live and let die,____ live and let die.____

Much faster ♩ = 154
Interlude:

Live and Let Die - 3 - 1

To Coda ⊕

Bridge:
w/reggae feel

Elec. Gtr. 1

mf

What does it mat - ter to ya, when you got a

job to do,___ you got - ta do it well,___ You got - ta

Live and Let Die - 3 - 2

give the oth - er fel - low hell!

MOONLIGHT

Words by
MARILYN BERGMAN and ALAN BERGMAN

Music by
JOHN WILLIAMS

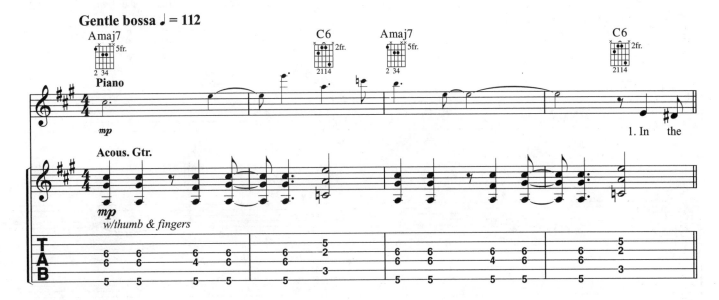

Verses 1 & 2:

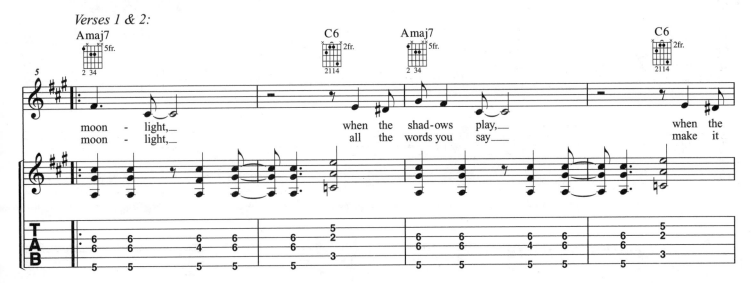

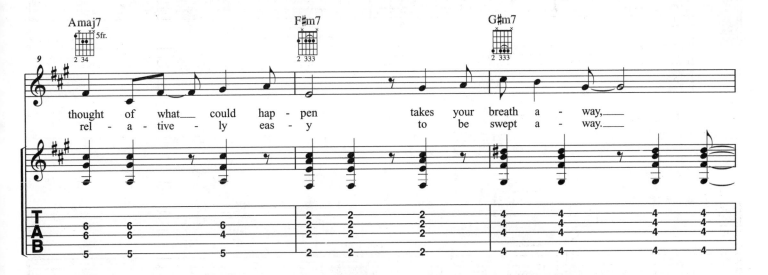

Moonlight - 3 - 1

LOOK WHAT YOU'VE DONE TO ME

Words and Music by
BOZ SCAGGS and DAVID FOSTER

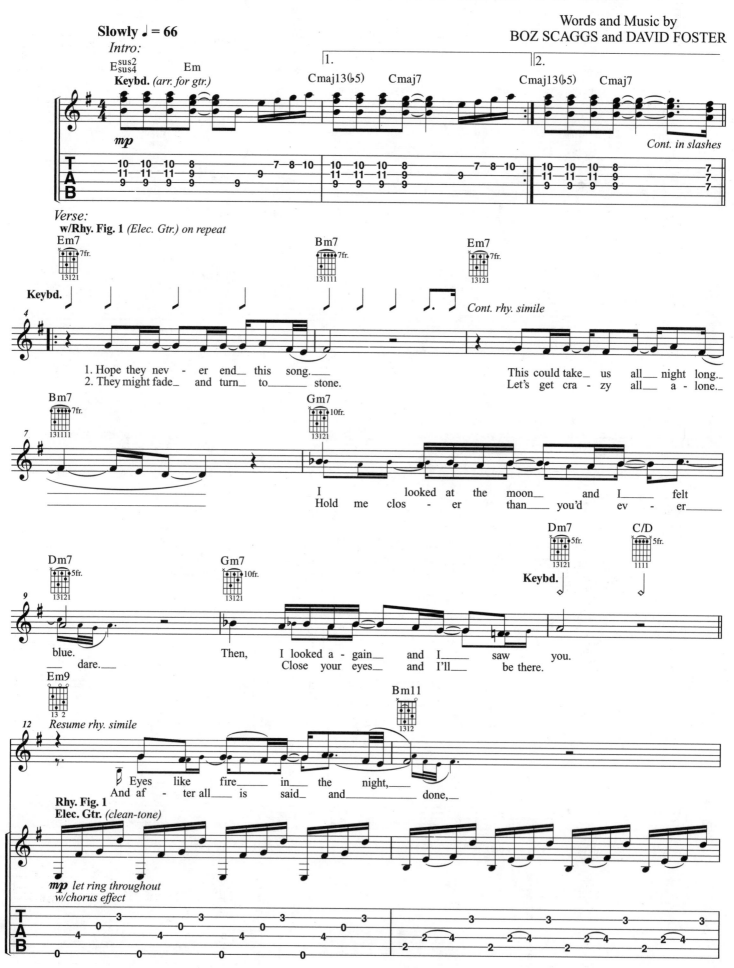

Look What You've Done to Me - 4 - 1

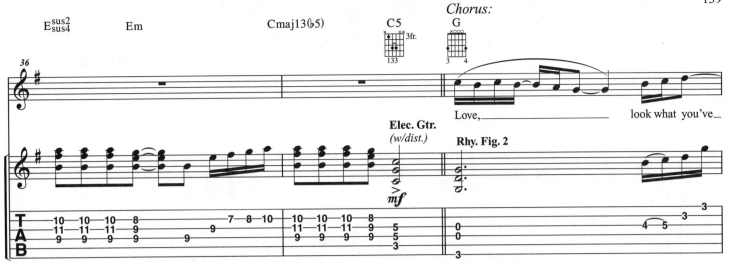

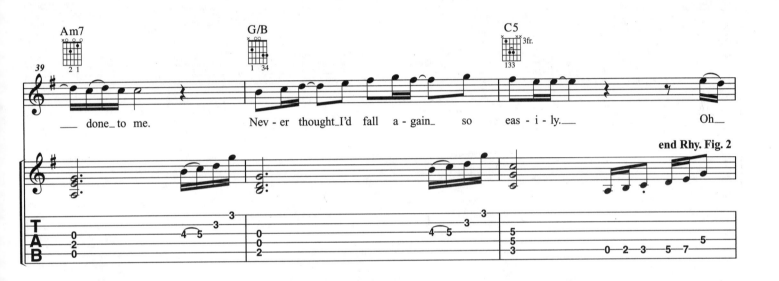

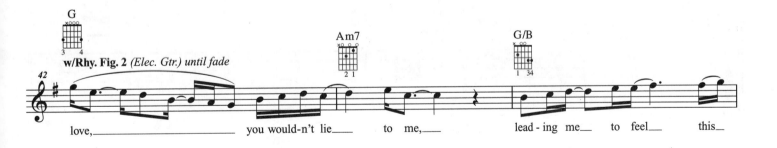

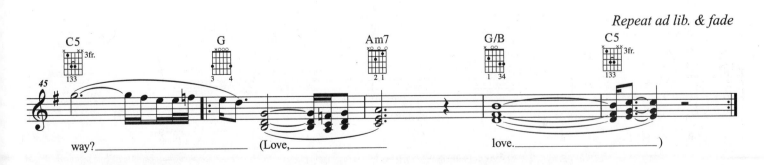

THE MAGNIFICENT SEVEN
(from *The Magnificent Seven*)

*To match record key, Capo I

By
ELMER BERNSTEIN

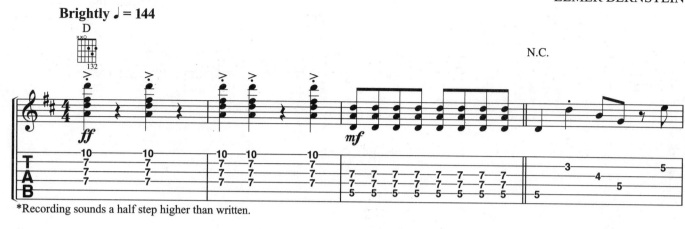

*Recording sounds a half step higher than written.

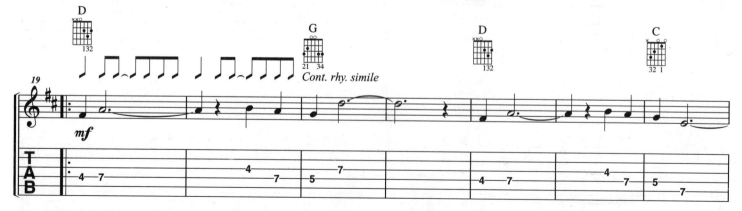

The Magnificent Seven - 2 - 1

The Magnificent Seven - 2 - 2

MISIRLOU

English Lyrics by
S.K. RUSSELL, FRED WISE and MILTON LEEDS

Music by
NICHOLAS ROUBANIS

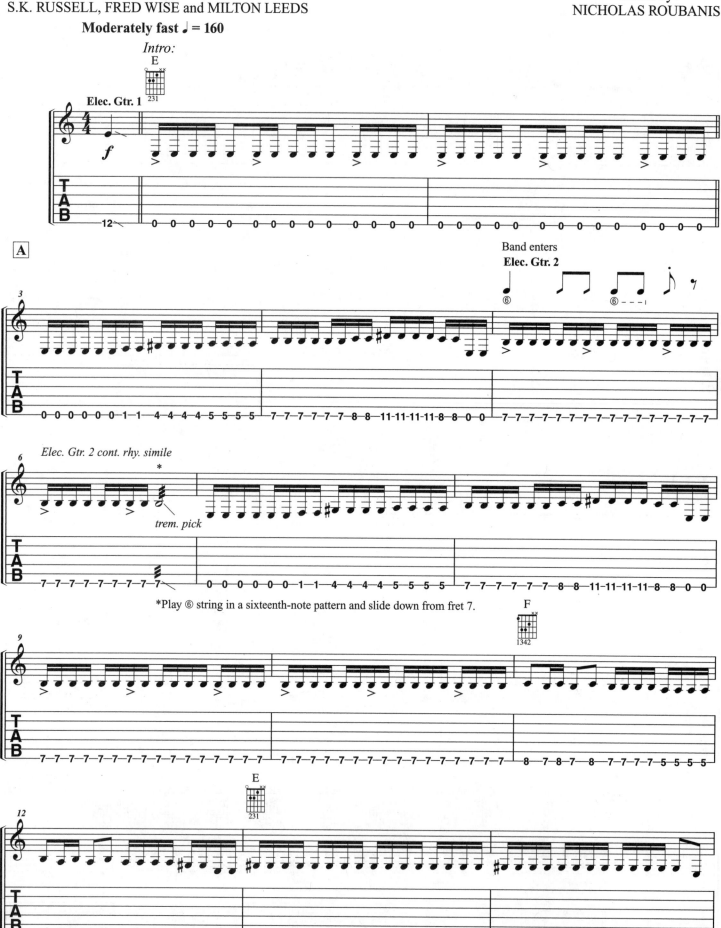

*Play ⑥ string in a sixteenth-note pattern and slide down from fret 7.

Misirlou - 4 - 1

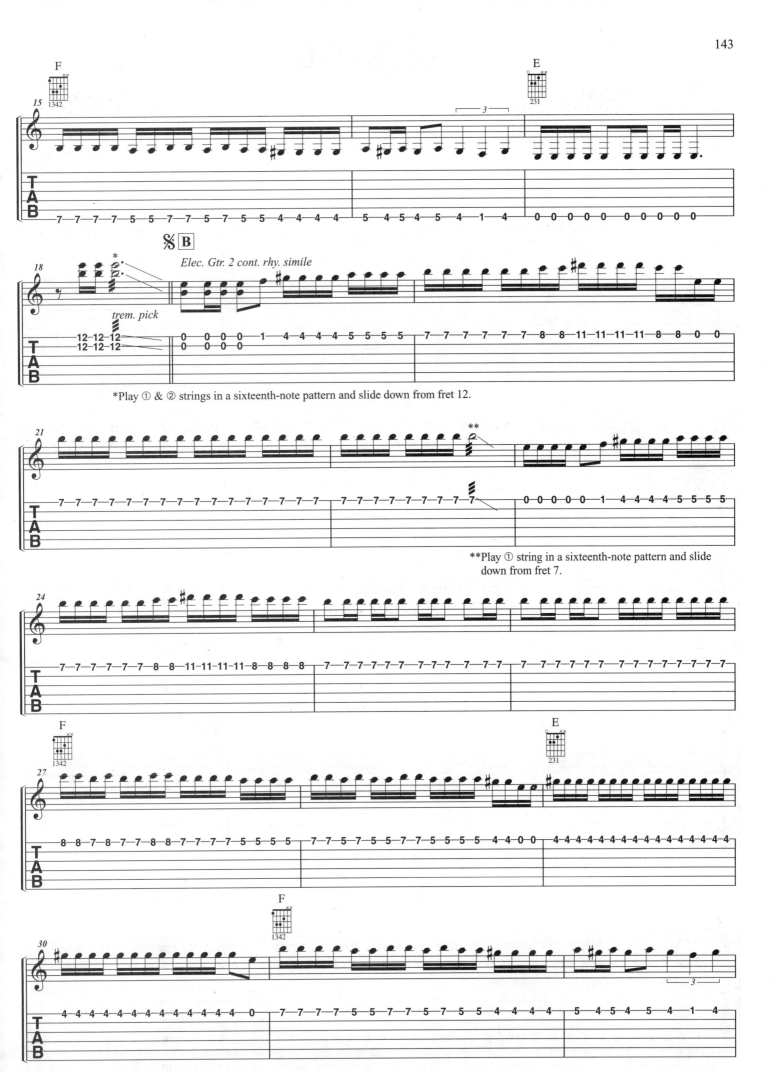

*Play ① & ② strings in a sixteenth-note pattern and slide down from fret 12.

**Play ① string in a sixteenth-note pattern and slide down from fret 7.

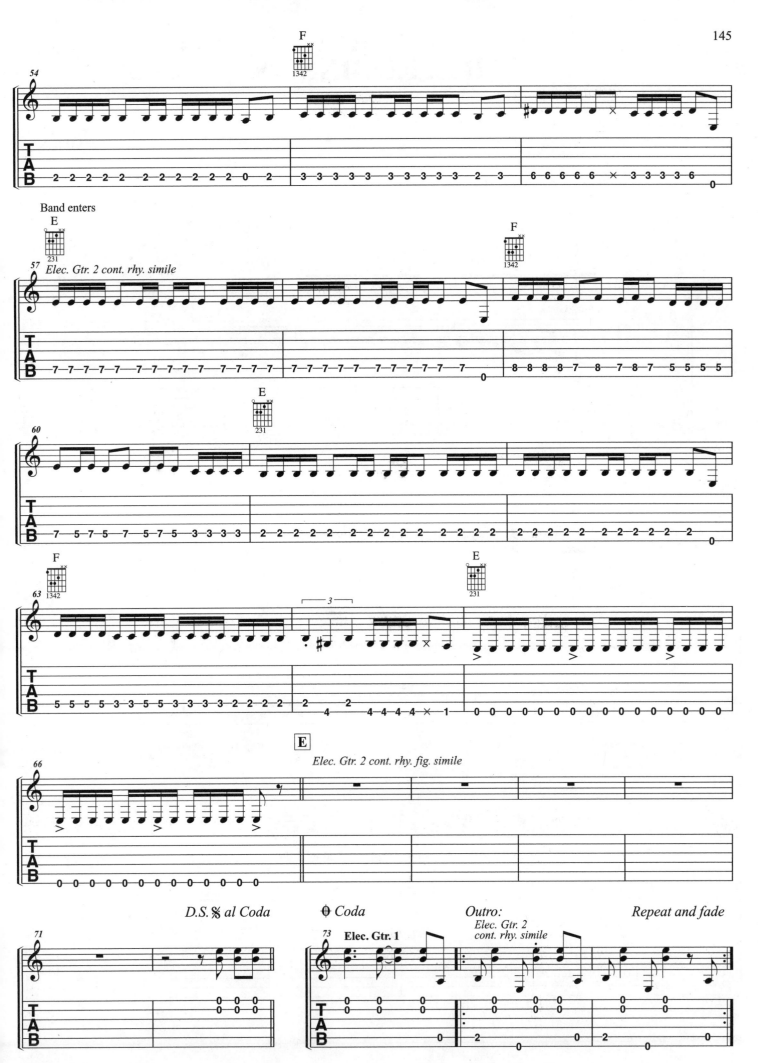

MRS. ROBINSON

To match record key, Capo II

Words and Music by
PAUL SIMON

Moderately bright ♩ = 104

Intro:

Dee   dee dee dee   dee   dee   dee dee   dee   dee   dee dee   dee.___

Do   do do do   do   do   do do do.___

Mrs. Robinson - 4 - 1

MY IMMORTAL

Words and Music by
BEN MOODY, AMY LEE and DAVID HODGES

*To match recording, Capo II

*Recording sounds a whole step higher than written.

1. I'm so tired of be-ing here,____

2. See additional lyrics

sup-pressed___ by all___ my child-ish fears._____ And if you have to leave,__

I wish that you would just___ leave, 'cause your pre-sence still lin-gers here,___

My Immortal - 3 - 1

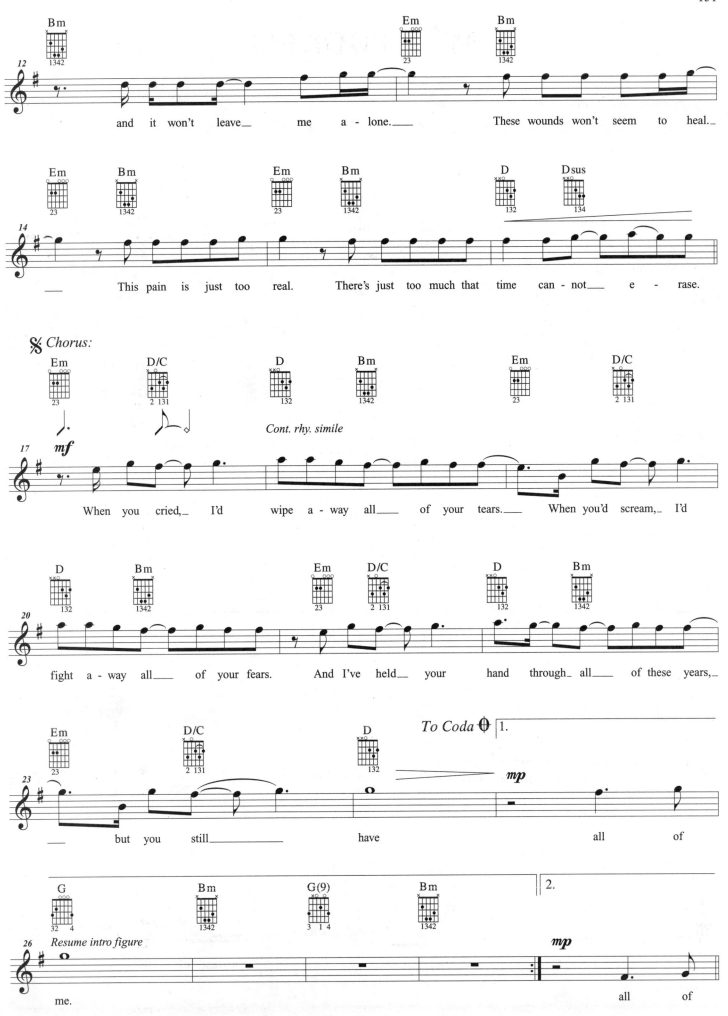

Bridge:

me.
I've tried___ so
hard to tell___ my - self that___ you're gone.
But
though you're___ still with___ me,___
I've been___ a -
lone all___ a - long.___

D.S. %% al Coda

Coda

Resume intro figure

all of me, all of me,___
___ all, me.

Verse 2:
You used to captivate me
By your resonating light.
But, now I'm bound by the life you left behind.
Your face, it haunts
My once pleasant dreams.
Your voice, it chased away
All the sanity in me.
These wounds won't seem to heal.
This pain is just too real.
There's just too much that time can not erase.

(To Chorus:)

NEVER ON SUNDAY

Lyrics by
BILLY TOWNE

Music by
MANOS HADJIDAKIS

Never on Sunday - 3 - 1

THEME FROM *NEW YORK, NEW YORK*

Words by
FRED EBB

Music by
JOHN KANDER

Theme from *New York, New York* - 3 - 1

NOBODY DOES IT BETTER

(from *The Spy Who Loved Me*)

Lyrics by
CAROLE BAYER SAGER

Music by
MARVIN HAMLISCH

OVER THE RAINBOW

Lyrics by
E.Y. HARBURG

Music by
HAROLD ARLEN

Over the Rainbow - 2 - 1

THE PINK PANTHER

(from *The Pink Panther*)

By
HENRY MANCINI

The Pink Panther - 2 - 1

The Pink Panther - 2 - 2

THE PRAYER

Italian Lyric by
ALBERTO TESTA and TONY RENIS

Words and Music by
CAROLE BAYER SAGER and DAVID FOSTER

*To match record key, Capo III

Slowly ♩ = 72

Intro:

*Recording sounds a minor 3rd higher than written.

I pray you'll be our

Verse 1:

eyes,   and watch us where we   go,   and help us to be

wise   in times when we don't   know._____   Let this be our

prayer,   when we lose our   way._____   Lead us to a place,

The Prayer - 4 - 1

Bridge:

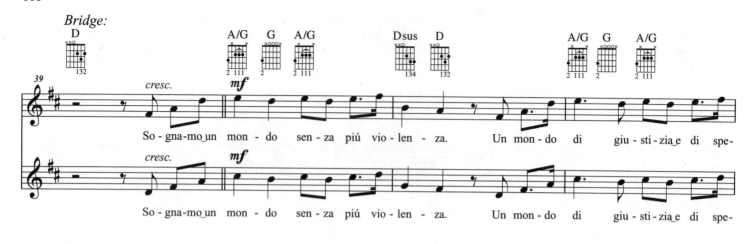

So - gna-mo_un mon - do sen - za piú vio - len - za. Un mon - do di giu - sti - zia_e di spe-

So - gna-mo_un mon - do sen - za piú vio - len - za. Un mon - do di giu - sti - zia_e di spe-

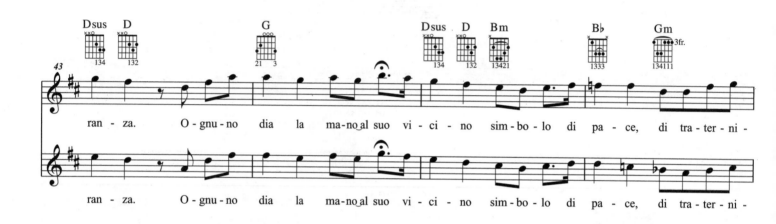

ran - za. O - gnu - no dia la ma-no_al suo vi - ci - no sim - bo - lo di pa - ce, di tra - ter - ni-

ran - za. O - gnu - no dia la ma-no_al suo vi - ci - no sim - bo - lo di pa - ce, di tra - ter - ni-

Verse 3:

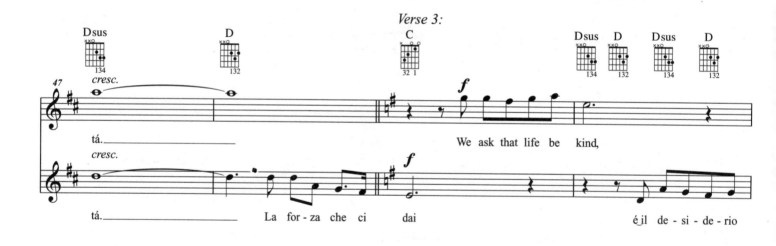

tá._____ We ask that life be kind,

tá._____ La for - za che ci dai é_il de - si - de - rio

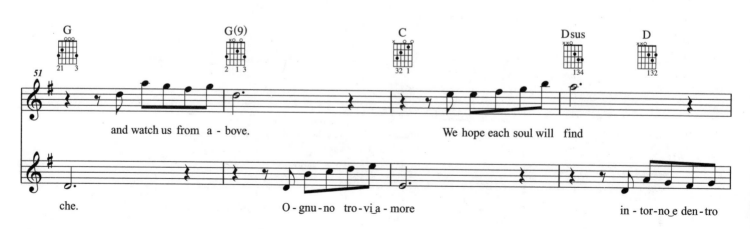

and watch us from a - bove. We hope each soul will find

che. O - gnu - no tro-vi_a - more in - tor-no_e den - tro

The Prayer - 4 - 3

(WE'RE GONNA)
ROCK AROUND THE CLOCK

Words and Music by
MAX C. FREEDMAN
and JIMMY DE KNIGHT

(We're Gonna) Rock Around the Clock - 4 - 1

172

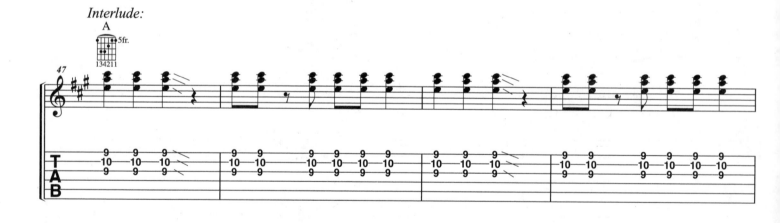

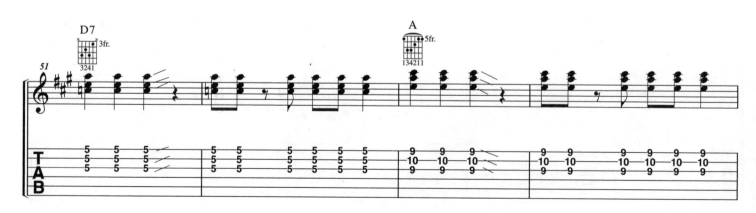

(We're Gonna) Rock Around the Clock - 4 - 3

(We're Gonna) Rock Around the Clock - 4 - 4

SCARBOROUGH FAIR/CANTICLE

*To match recording, Capo VII

Arrangement and original counter melody by
PAUL SIMON and ARTHUR GARFUNKEL

*Recording sounds a three whole steps higher than written.

*Harmony sung on D.S. only.

Scarborough Fair/Canticle - 4 - 1

176

SEPARATE LIVES

Words and Music by
STEPHEN BISHOP

Separate Lives - 4 - 1

THE SHADOW OF YOUR SMILE

(from *The Sandpiper*)

Lyrics by
PAUL FRANCIS WEBER

Music by
JOHNNY MANDEL

SINGIN' IN THE RAIN
(from *Singin' in the Rain*)

Lyric by
ARTHUR FREED

Music by
NACIO HERB BROWN

Singin' in the Rain - 3 - 1

Singin' in the Rain - 3 - 3

SHE

*To match record key, Capo I

Words and Music by
CHARLES AZNAVOUR and
HERBERT KRETZMER

Slowly ♩ = 65

Intro:

*Recording sounds a half step higher than written.

Verse 1:

She___ may be the face I can't for - get,___ a trace of plea - sure or re - gret,___ may be the trea - sure or the

price___ I have to pay. She___ may be the song that sum - mer sings,___ may be the still that aut - umn

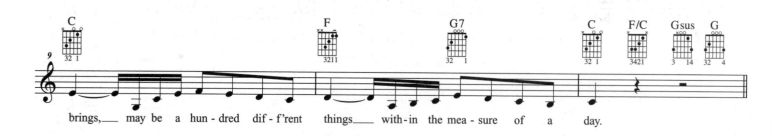

brings,___ may be a hun - dred dif - f'rent things___ with - in the mea - sure of a day.

𝄋 *Verses 2–4:*

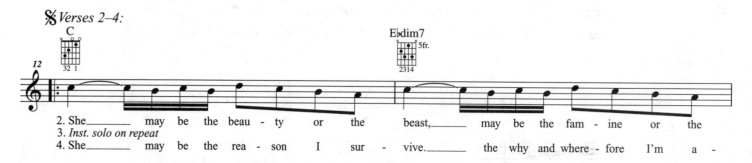

2. She___ may be the beau - ty or the beast,___ may be the fam - ine or the
3. *Inst. solo on repeat*
4. She___ may be the rea - son I sur - vive.___ the why and where - fore I'm a -

She - 2 - 1

feast,_____ my turn each day in-to a heav-en or a hell.
live,_____ the one I'll care for through the rough_____ and read-y years.

She_____ may be the mir-ror of my dream,_____ a smile re-flec-ted in a
Me,_____ I'll take here laugh-ter and her tears_____ and make them all my sou-ve-

To Coda

stream,_____ she may not be what she may seem in-side her shell.
nirs_____ for where she goes I've got to

2. *Bridge:*

She_____ who al-ways seems so hap-py in a crowd,_____ whose eyes can be so pri-vate and so

proud,_____ no-one's al-lowed to see them when they cry. She_____ may be the love that can-not hope to

D.S. % al Coda

last,_____ may come to me from shad-ows of the past_____ that I re-mem-ber 'til the day I die.

Coda

be,_____ the mean-ing of my life is she, she,_____ she.

She - 2 - 2

SOMEWHERE, MY LOVE
(LARA'S THEME)

(from Doctor Zhivago)

Lyric by
PAUL FRANCIS WEBSTER

Music by
MAURICE JARRE

Moderately fast but gentle waltz ♩ = 180

trem. picking throughout

Cont. rhy. simile

Verse 1:

Some - where, my love,_____ there will be songs to sing,_____

al - though the snow_____ cov - ers the hope of spring.

Some - where a hill_____ blos-soms in green and gold,_____

and there are dreams,_____ all that your heart can hold.

Somewhere, My Love (Lara's Theme) - 2 - 1

STREETS OF PHILADELPHIA

Moderately ♩ = 96

Intro:

Words and Music by
BRUCE SPRINGSTEEN

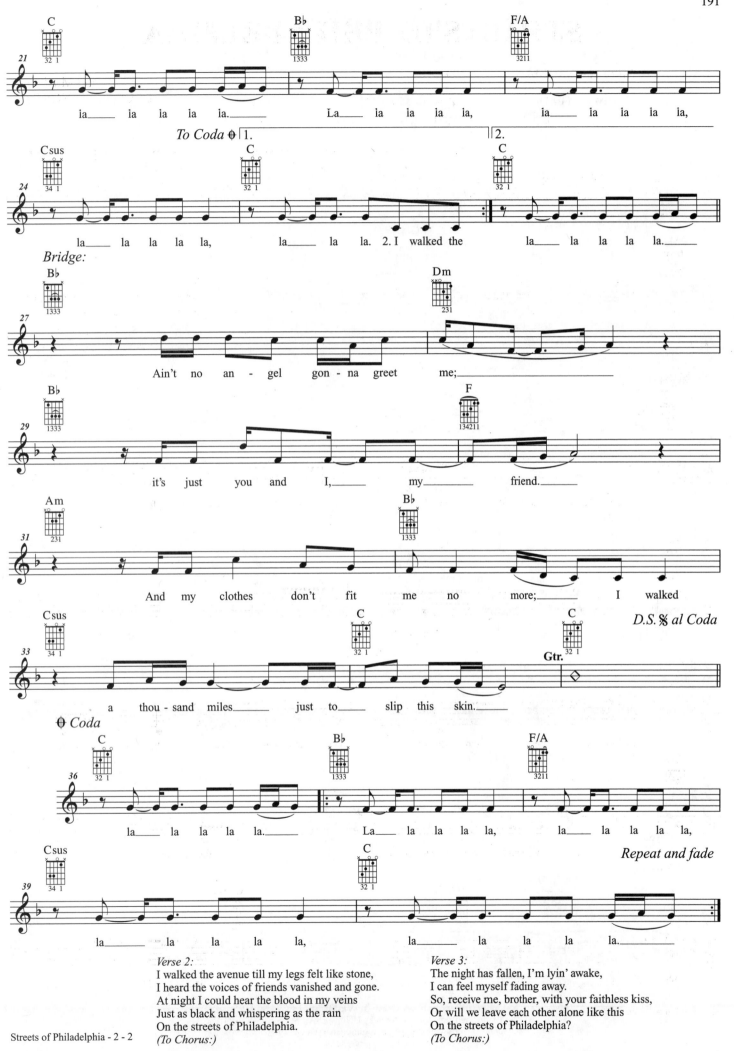

Verse 2:
I walked the avenue till my legs felt like stone,
I heard the voices of friends vanished and gone.
At night I could hear the blood in my veins
Just as black and whispering as the rain
On the streets of Philadelphia.
(To Chorus:)

Verse 3:
The night has fallen, I'm lyin' awake,
I can feel myself fading away.
So, receive me, brother, with your faithless kiss,
Or will we leave each other alone like this
On the streets of Philadelphia?
(To Chorus:)

THE SUMMER KNOWS

(Theme from *The Summer of '42*)

Lyrics by
ALAN and MARILYN BERGMAN

Music by
MICHEL LEGRAND

THEME FROM *ICE CASTLES*
(Through the Eyes of Love)

Lyrics by
CAROLE BAYER SAGER

Music by
MARVIN HAMLISCH

Theme from *Ice Castles* (Through the Eyes of Love) - 3 - 1

194

THEME FROM *ZORBA THE GREEK*

(Zorba's Dance)

By
MIKAS THEODORAKIS

Slowly with a cut-time feel ♩ = 72

Theme from *Zorba the Greek* - 5 - 1

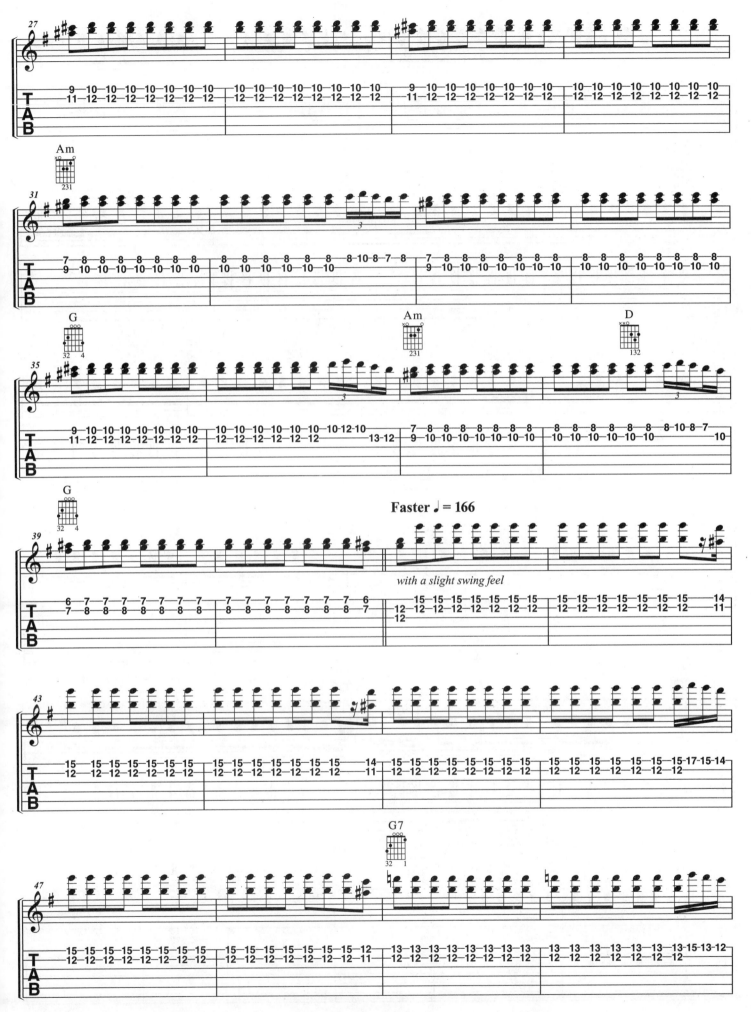

Theme from *Zorba the Greek* - 5 - 2

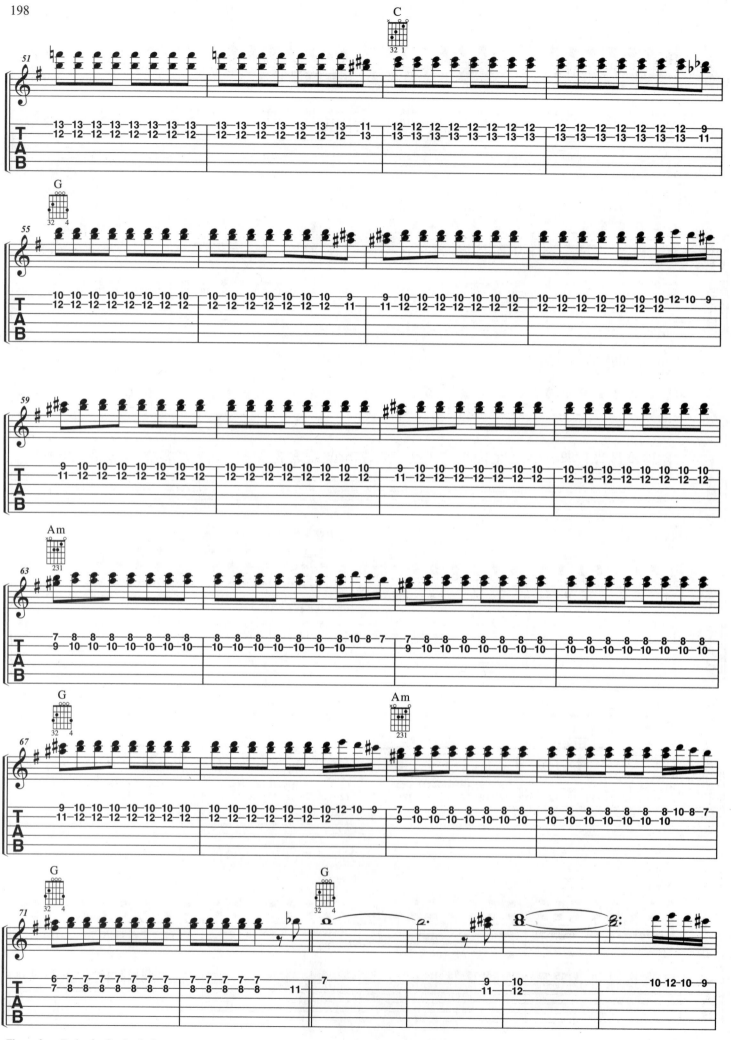

Theme from *Zorba the Greek* - 5 - 3

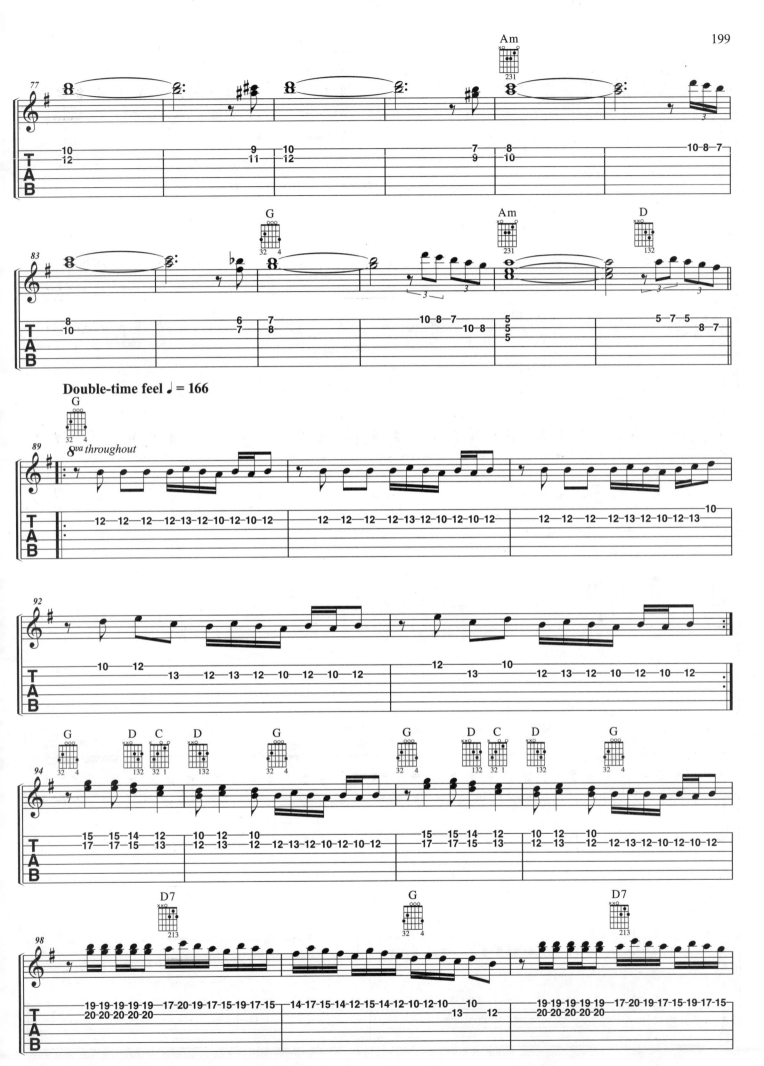

Theme from *Zorba the Greek* - 5 - 4

Theme from *Zorba the Greek* - 5 - 5

THERE YOU'LL BE

(from *Pearl Harbor*)

*To match record key, Capo I

Words and Music by
DIANE WARREN

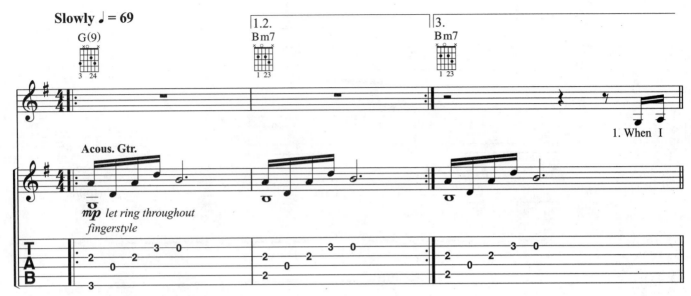

*Recording sounds a half step higher than written.

There You'll Be - 3 - 1

There You'll Be - 3 - 2

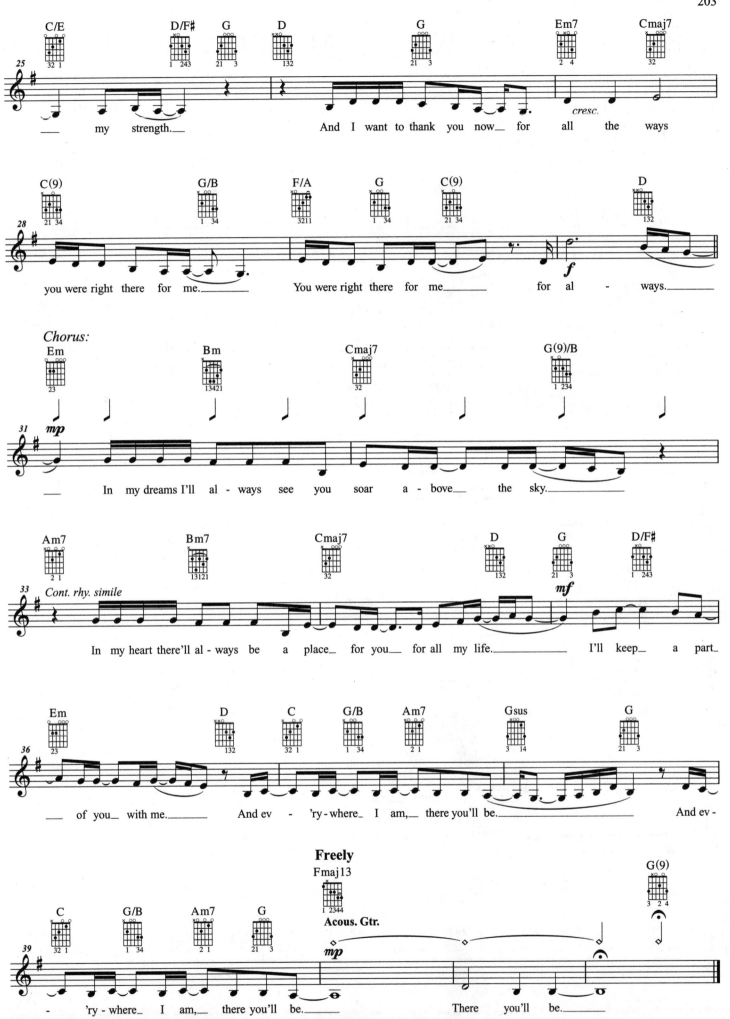

There You'll Be - 3 - 3

TOWN WITHOUT PITY

Lyric by
NED WASHINGTON

Music by
DIMITRI TIOMKIN

Town Without Pity - 4 - 1

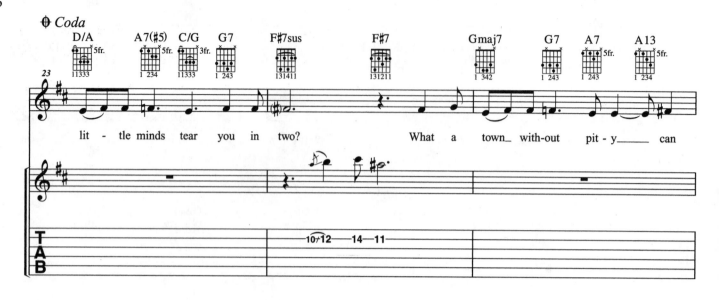

lit - tle minds tear you in two? What a town_ with-out pit - y_____ can

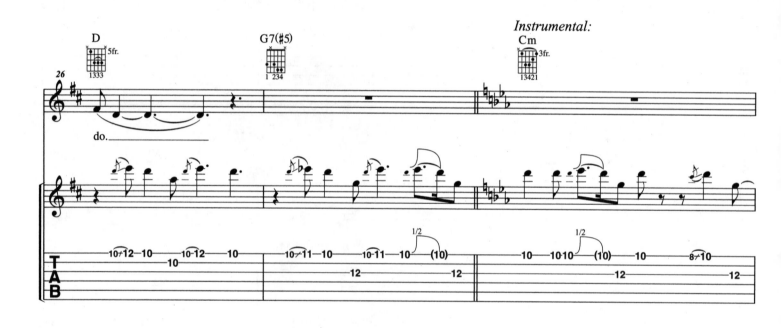

do._____

Instrumental:

How_ can

Town Without Pity - 4 - 4

WHAT'S NEW PUSSYCAT?

Words by
HAL DAVID

Music by
BURT BACHARACH

THE WINDMILLS OF YOUR MIND

(from *The Thomas Crown Affair*)

Words by
ALAN and MARILYN BERGMAN

Music by
MICHEL LEGRAND

The Windmills of Your Mind - 4 - 1

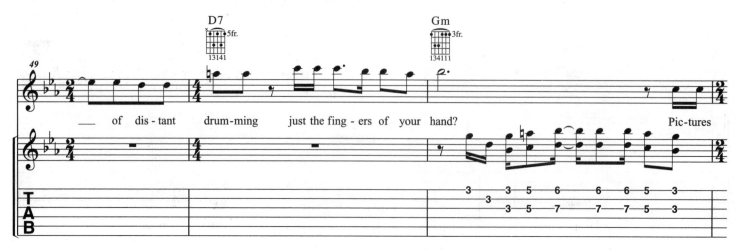

The Windmills of Your Mind - 4 - 4

YOU'RE A MEAN ONE, MR. GRINCH

(from Dr. Seuss' *How the Grinch Stole Christmas*)

Lyric by
DR. SUESS

Music by
ALBERT HAGUE

You're a Mean One, Mr. Grinch - 2 - 1

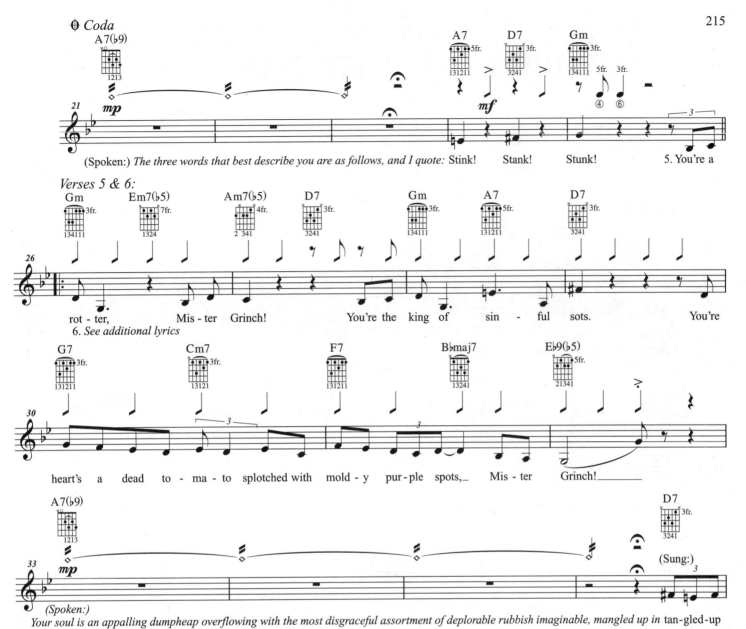

⊕ *Coda*

(Spoken:) *The three words that best describe you are as follows, and I quote:* Stink! Stank! Stunk! 5. You're a

Verses 5 & 6:

rot - ter, Mis - ter Grinch! You're the king of sin - ful sots. You're

6. *See additional lyrics*

heart's a dead to - ma - to splotched with mold - y pur - ple spots,__ Mis - ter Grinch!_____

(Sung:)

(Spoken:)
Your soul is an appalling dumpheap overflowing with the most disgraceful assortment of deplorable rubbish imaginable, mangled up in tan-gled-up

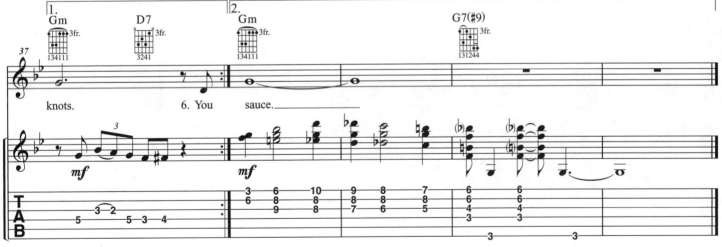

knots. 6. You sauce._____

Verse 2:
You're a monster, Mr. Grinch! Your heart's an empty hole.
Your brain is full of spiders, you've got garlic in your soul, Mr. Grinch!
I wouldn't touch you with a thirty-nine-and-a-half-foot pole.

Verse 3:
You're a vile one, Mr. Grinch! You have termites in your smile.
You have all the tender sweetness of a seasick crocodile, Mr. Grinch!
(Spoken:) And given the choice between the two of you,
(Sung:) I'd take the seasick crocodile

You're a Mean One, Mr. Grinch - 2 - 2

Verse 4:
You're a foul one, Mr. Grinch! You're a nasty-wasty skunk!
Your heart is full of unwashed socks, your soul is full of gunk, Mr. Grinch!
(Spoken:) The three words that best describe you are as follows, and I quote:
(Sung:) Stink! Stank! Stunk!
(To Verse 5:)

Verse 6:
You nauseate me, Mr. Grinch! With a nauseous, super naus.
You're a crooked jerky jockey and you drive a crooked hoss, Mr. Grinch!
(Spoken:) You're a three-decker Sauerkraut and toadstool sandwich
(Sung:) …with arsenic sauce.

YOU'VE GOT A FRIEND IN ME

(from *Toy Story*)

*To match recording, Capo I

Words and Music by
RANDY NEWMAN

Easy shuffle ♩ = 108

Intro:

D F♯7/C♯ Bm B♭7 D/A A7 D C♯/A C/A C♯/A

Cont. rhy. simile

mf

Recording sounds a half step higher than written.

Verses 1 & 2:

D C♯/A D9 G G♯dim7 D

1. You've got a friend in me._____ You've got a friend in me._____
2. You've got a friend in me._____ You've got a friend in me._____

G D/F♯ F♯7/C♯ Bm G D/F♯ F♯7/C♯ Bm

When the road_ looks rough a - head_ and you're miles_ and miles_____ from your nice_ warm bed._
You got trou - bles, *then* I got 'em_ too._____ There is - n't an - y - thing I would - n't do_____ for you.

G C♯/G♯ D/A F♯/A♯ G7 F♯7 Bm E7 A7 D B7

You just re - mem - ber what your old pal said, boy, you've_ got a friend in me.____ Yeah, you've_
If we stick to - geth - er we can see it through, 'cause you've_ got a friend in me.____ Yeah, you've_

You've Got a Friend in Me - 2 - 1

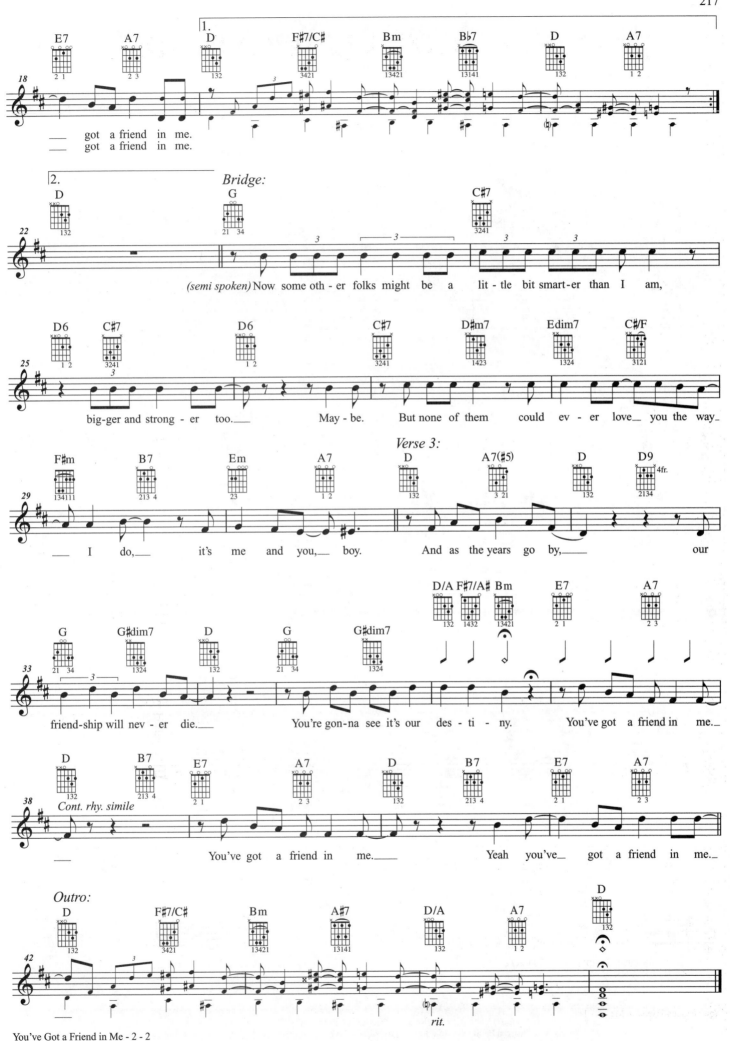

WOODSTOCK

Moderately ♩ = 112

Intro:

Words and Music by
JONI MITCHELL

*Elec. Gtrs. 1 & 2 simile on repeats.

Chorus:

Outro:

Cont. rhy. simile

Verse 2:

Well, then can I walk beside you? I have come to lose the smog.
And I feel as if a cog in something turning.
And maybe it's the time of year, yes, and maybe it's the time of man.
And I don't know who I am but life is for learning.
(To Chorus:)

Verse 3:

By the time we got to Woodstock, we were half a million strong,
And everywhere was a song and a celebration.
And I dreamed I saw the bomber jet planes riding shotgun in the sky,
Turning into butterflies above our nation.
(To Chorus:)